The Joy of Serving Widows

A guide to beginning a Widow and
Homebound Ministry in your church

by
Vicki Hendryx

TOD
PRESS

Published in the United States of America
by TOD Press

(a division of TATE PUBLISHING, LLC)

All Scripture references are King James Version,
unless otherwise indicated.

Printed in the United States of America by

TATE PUBLISHING, LLC

1716 West State Highway 152

Mustang, OK 73064

(888) 361-9473

Publisher's Cataloging in Publication

Hendryx, Vicki

The Joy of Serving Widows/Vicki Hendryx

Originally published in Mustang,OK:TATE PUBLISHING:2004

1. Christianity 2. Church ministries 3. Senior adults

ISBN 0-9753933-1-6 $11.95

First Printing: May 2004

Since you call on a Father who judges each man's work impartially, live your lives as strangers here in reverent fear. For you know that it was not with perishable things such as silver or gold that you were redeemed from the empty way of life handed down to you from your forefathers, but with the precious blood of Christ, a lamb without blemish or defect. He was chosen before the creation of the world, but was revealed in these last times for your sake. Through him you believe in God, who raised him from the dead and glorified him, and so your faith and hope are in God. Now that you have purified yourselves by obeying the truth so that you have sincere love for your brothers, **love one another deeply, from the heart**. For you have been born again, not of perishable seed, but of imperishable, through the living and enduring word of God.

1 Peter 1:17-23

INDEX

APPENDIX

IN THE BEGINNING

I have started many new projects in my lifetime… it's a shame I haven't finished them all. Because of my personality, gifts and for whatever reason God made me the way I am, I really need and enjoy short-term projects. It is for this very reason that I can tell you, I did not start this widow's ministry - God did. **Philippians 1:6 says this, "being confident of this, that he who began a good work in you will carry it on to completion until the day of Christ Jesus."** God gave me this plan for a widow/widower ministry in our church in 1998, and it is still alive and active in the First Baptist Church of Skiatook, Oklahoma today.

The Joy of Serving Widows is a training manual designed to lead you step-by-step into a church-wide ministry connecting widows and homebound with families in your church. Each widow will be "adopted" by a family or Sunday School class ranging from Adults, to teens, to children's classes. This network of love honors God and is a very real witness to each widow's family members and neighbors. The prayer cover in your church grows as families and widows are praying for each other. Widows are taught that no matter what their age or state of health, they can still serve God and live a useful abundant life.

God has given me a special love for older people. I am hyper; they are calm. I cannot sit still; they sit for long periods of time. I can talk a lot and say little; they can talk little and say a lot. They are everything I am not, but will become in time. I have lived my whole life in Skiatook, Oklahoma and have watched ladies, and a few men, in our community and churches grow older and widowed. Some are very active and others seem to sit and wait their turn to die. I believe this is directly related to their spiritual walk with the Lord. Jesus said in **John 10:10 [KJV], "I am come that they might have life, and that they might have it more abundantly."** He did not say, "until you are old and then no one cares anymore." God wants to bless all His children, love them and use them no matter what their ages. Senior saints have so much wisdom and love to share, and time to share it, but few to share it with. Young women, we have so many things we could learn from older women. A woman in her 70's volunteered to teach a quilting class in our church twice a month. I have learned so much from her and have made three quilts for my family using old clothes. What a blessing. Have you ever sat in a prayer circle while an elderly woman prayed for you? I have and it was such a blessing and inspiration listening to what she prayed and the way she prayed after 70+ years of experience talking to God. And I'll never forget the way a hush and expectancy fell all around us listening to Brother Willard Kern in his deep voice, call out, "Father...Father..., it's me again." Oh how much we have to learn from men and women who have lived on this earth depending on God over and over throughout their lifetimes.

In May of 1998, were studying the story of the good Samaritan in our couples' Sunday School Class when a friend said, "Sometimes we see a need, but are just too busy to stop and do anything about it." How many times have you thought that you needed to do something for someone, but never got around to it? We must put feet to our faith and obey His calling when we hear God telling us to do something.

James 2:14-17 [NKJ], "14What does it profit, my brethren, if someone says he has faith but does not have works? Can faith save him? 15If a brother or sister is naked and destitute of daily food, 16and one of you says to them, "Depart in peace, be warmed and filled," but you do not give them the things which are needed for the body, what does it profit? 17Thus also faith by itself, if it does not have works, is dead.

Now we know that **Ephesians 2:8-10 says, "8For it is by grace you have been saved, through faith – and this not from yourselves, it is the gift of God – 9not by works, so that no one can boast. 10For we are God's workmanship, created in Christ Jesus to do good works, which God prepared in advance for us to do."** Did you see that? God prepared in advance good works for us to do. HA. Never again do you have to sit and watch mindless television and be bored. And we are reminded in verse 9 that works do not save us. We are saved by the grace of God when we believe and call on the name of Jesus, who was sent to show us the Father. **"The Word became flesh and made his dwelling among us. We have seen his glory, the glory of the One and Only, who came from the Father, full of grace and truth." John 1:14** I believe Jesus was born of a virgin; died on the cross as the perfect lamb of God; His shed blood paid the penalty for my sins and the sins of the world and provided forgiveness that redeemed my soul; He rose again and now stands at the right hand of the Father making intercession for me. Oh Glory. I have been bought and paid for at great price and I am redeemed. Eternal life is the gift of God. My gift back to Him is what I do with that life. What are you doing with the life God gave you? Good intentions are nothing without action, so let's get to work!

After the Lord got my attention that Sunday, through a series of events over a two-week period, He laid it on my heart to start a widow's ministry. One of the first things I did was call our pastor and share with him the excitement of what God was leading me to do, and I sought his endorsement. I believe the pastor of each church has been placed as a leader over the flock and sometimes works as sort of a "checks and balances" system. He can confirm and give his blessings or raise some important questions if he sees a red flag. My pastor said to go right ahead and run with it, and that's just what I did.

If you are being led by the Lord to begin this ministry in your church, let me encourage you to go first to your pastor and share this program with him. He may have had others come to him with the same burden for the elderly in your church. Then you have confirmation and a support group you didn't even know existed.

My prayer for you is that this book will be the spark that lights your fire.

ONE-ON-ONE

We have been adopted into the family of God. **Romans 8:14-16, "[14]because those who are led by the Spirit of God are sons of God. [15]For you did not receive a spirit that makes you a slave again to fear, but you received the Spirit of sonship [or adoption]. And by him we cry, Abba Father. [16]The Spirit himself testifies with our spirit that we are God's children."** As I read this verse, I thought about how wonderful it is to be wanted and loved by God and adopted into His family. Then God spoke to my heart that widows needed to be wanted and loved and adopted into our families. This great Almighty God who created the universe is also a very personal God who desires a one-on-one relationship with us.

Jesus touched people's lives one-on-one. When the crowds surrounded him for healing, he could have looked out over the crowd and healed the entire group at once, but he did not. He touched them one by one.

- **Luke 4:40, "When the sun was setting, the people brought to Jesus all who had various kinds of sickness, and laying his hands on each one, he healed them."**
- **Matthew 8:3, "Jesus reached out his hand and touched the man..."**

- **Matthew 8:15, "He touched her hand and the fever left her..."**
- **Matthew 9:29, "Then he touched their eyes..."**
- **Matthew 17:7, "But Jesus came and touched them..."**
- **Mark 1:41, "Filled with compassion, Jesus reached out his hand and touched the man..."**

We must reach out to widows, not just as a group, but one by one and touch their lives just as Jesus reaches out and touches our lives one by one and calls us by name.

A widow has lost the daily one-on-one relationship she had with her spouse, and this has left a great void in her life. She goes to church and sits among people, but how many people stop to touch her life? Who knows anything about her? Have you ever felt the pangs of sitting alone in a crowd? I have. I cannot imagine living that way week after week.

Isolation is one of the biggest problems surrounding a widow. Her life was once busy raising children, visiting with other mothers, volunteering at school functions, working outside the home, singing in the church choir, teaching a Sunday School class, cooking food for funeral dinners, sharing meals with a sick friend, bowling on a league, working with cub scouts and girl scouts, gardening, fishing, entertaining guests and sharing it all with her loving husband. Now her life is reduced to hopefully seeing one of her children live nearby who will bring in groceries and take her to the doctor. Isolation has descended on her, and it brings with it depression, fear, loneliness and hopelessness. The love of God brings new life, new family, new love and fresh hope. Let the Lord use you today to bring a refreshing wind of love through His Spirit into the lives of the widows or homebound in your church family.

Through the "adoption" process set out in this book, people are connected one-on-one, and the widow is no longer a small old person lost in the crowd. She is someone special who is sought out, spoken to, touched, hugged, loved on, ministered to and sat with at church.

I must stop here and tell you I use the term "widow" to signify interchangeably either widow or widower. It is just that out of 34 widows in our church, only two are males. So it is easier for me to use the term "widow" with the understanding that this covers men also.

The Joy of Serving Widows

AND NOW YOU

Have you felt God calling you to serve Him? If God is leading you to begin a widow's ministry in your church, there are several basic principles you should consider.

WHAT DOES THE BIBLE SAY ABOUT WIDOWS?

James 1:27 says, "Religion that God our Father accepts as pure and faultless is this: to look after orphans and widows in their distress and to keep oneself from being polluted by the world."

The very essence of God is love. In 1 Peter 1:22, we are told to love one another deeply, from the heart. **Isaiah 46:4** says, **"Even to your old age and gray hairs I am he, I am he who will sustain you. I have made you and I will carry you; I will sustain you and I will rescue you."** Widows, as a group, need to be told that God has not forgotten them, not to be afraid, and that God loves them and cares for them. They are distressed from all the news of war and threats of terrorism they hear on television and need someone to comfort and reassure them. I suggest to you to reassure them with scripture of God's love and care. Type or print IN LARGE LETTERS scriptures like Isaiah 46:4 and put it on an index card they can tape to their refrigerator door or lay on a table near their bed or chair. When they are afraid, they will find reassurance in God's Word.

In Acts chapter 6, we read that one of the first organized

activities of the New Testament church was feeding and caring for widows. The disciples chose Stephen, a man full of faith and the Holy Spirit to oversee this program. Let me encourage you also to read all of 1Timothy 5, which has much to say about the care of widows. **1Timothy 5:3-6 says, "Give proper recognition to those widows who are really in need. But if a widow has children or grandchildren, these should learn first of all to put their religion into practice by caring for their own family and so repaying their parents and grandparents, for this is pleasing to God. The widow who is really in need and left all alone puts her hope in God and continues night and day to pray and to ask God for help."** In our society today, so mobile with families spread all across the globe, we see too often widows with no family in the town or even the state where they live. These widows really need more attention and help.

HOW DO I FIND THE WIDOWS IN MY CHURCH?

I went to each Sunday School teacher or secretary of each class involving people who were 60 years old and above. I asked them to go through their rolls and make a list of everyone who was widowed. Since our church has two Sunday morning services, I don't always know who joins the church. Periodically I call the church office and ask them if they know of any new members who fit this category.

Another good source is the widows themselves. They

keep me informed of any new members or friends who are widowed.

WHO SHOULD BE INCLUDED?

1 Timothy 5: 9-10, tells us **"No widow may be put on the list of widows <u>unless she is over sixty</u>, has been faithful to her husband, and is well known for her good deeds, such as bringing up children, showing hospitality, washing the feet of the saints, helping those in trouble and devoting herself to all kinds of good deeds.**

You will find that some widows have lots of family living close by and some even live in the same household with their children. Now consider the difference in needs between that widow and a widow who has no family in the entire state. That is why I try to follow the instructions found in 1 Timothy 5:8-10. If they have family living in the same town as they do, then that is wonderful. But even a family member who loves their widowed mother, father, or grandparent, needs a break sometimes. It can become very burdensome to be the sole caretaker. How nice if someone from your church called and said they would like to spend a couple of hours that day with a widow who has Alzheimer or bring in a meal. Another need to consider is from the viewpoint of the widow. Everyone they are in contact with loves them because they "have to" because they are family. They need to be loved by someone who loves them just for who they are and because of God's love.

Depending on the size of your church, you may be able

to put every widow who is 60 years old and above on the list or expand it even further. But if you have a very large church, you may need to narrow that using certain stipulations:

a.   **Widows who are 65 or 70 and above;**
b.   **With no family in your town;**
c.   **Who cannot drive; or**
d.   **Who have physical limitations**

When I first started putting a list together, another question that arose several times was, "Well, I am divorced and that is like being a widow, so why won't you put me on the list." First of all, that covers a whole different ministry. A divorced person has some very complex emotional, spiritual, physical and sociological needs that differ from a 70-year-old widow. And second, I always rely on the Bible for guidelines. I simply, and lovingly, ask them if they meet the criteria set out in 1 Timothy 5:8-10. For me and our church at the time, I had to draw the line somewhere, and what better standard than the Bible for "rightly dividing the word of truth." (2 Timothy 2:15)

FIRST THINGS FIRST

I am a judicial secretary/legal assistant and I love organization and forms, mostly because I have such a memory defect that I either have to have yellow sticky post-its everywhere (and I do mean everywhere) or I must make a form. Hence, I came up with a Widow Profile. **[Widow Profile - Appendix 1]** The fun part is in taking this form to each home and visiting with the widows. They love the attention and the thought of someone caring enough about them to come to their house. One lady told me this was the first time in six years that anyone from church had come to visit her. They also love talking about their families, so I always try to ask how they first met their husbands. Oh how their eyes light up as they remember the love they shared.

Widows and widowers have a real need to talk about the death of their spouse. Some will cry... but it is very healing. This will give you an opportunity to minister to them, put your arm around them, love them and pray with them. Many times family members are tired of hearing about it and tired of their parent or grandparent crying. They tell them coldly to get over it and move on. One of the best ways I've found to deal with a widow's sorrow and grief is to let them talk about the good times they shared together and ask them to tell a funny story. Then I remind them that their husband or wife wouldn't want them to spend the rest of their life sad and grieving. They shared so much joy and happiness, that they would want the other to be happy again. God has a way of bringing the joy and laughter back into their lives when they are willing to ask Him. Healing takes time and at first they may even feel guilty about having a happy moment. Our God is the God of Joy. Share with them scriptures about joy, such as:

Psalm 16:11, "In thy presence is fullness of joy; at thy right hand are pleasures for evermore."

Psalm 103:1-5, "Praise the Lord, O my soul; all my inmost being, praise his holy name. Praise the Lord, O my soul, and forget not all his benefits – who forgives all your sins and heals all your diseases, who redeems your life from the pit and crowns you with love and compassion, who satisfies your desires with good things so that your youth is renewed like the eagle's."

Psalm 118:24, "This is the day the Lord has made. We will rejoice and be glad in it." Are you rejoicing today? Each day is a gift from God and you should honor Him by thanking him for your day. Get up and declare that you are happy today. Say it out loud. Speak positive words out loud. Focus on the positive. Turn to someone or look in the mirror and say, "I feel great and it's going to be a wonderful day because this is the day the Lord has made. I will rejoice and be glad in it." It is very uplifting to start your day praising God.

Maybe they need to get things right with God and get a fresh start. **Psalm 51:7-14** talks about spiritual cleansing and prayer to "restore the joy of my salvation."

Nehemiah 8:10 says, "...the joy of the Lord is your

strength." and **Proverbs 17:22**, tells us a cheerful heart is good medicine.

The next visit, I take a Joy Box. I wrap a shoe box in bright happy paper and tape a scripture about joy on the top. Then I tell her that from this day forward she is to start collecting little things in life that make her smile like she did when she was a little girl - a picture, a flower, a birthday card, etc. As her box fills up, her grief disappears. She starts to have an attitude of gratitude and realize there are many things that can bring her happiness.

WIDOW / WIDOWER/ HOMEBOUND / PROFILE

On this form you will of course need basic information: name, address, telephone, birthday. I've also included a space for directions to their house. Many times they live in meandering apartment complexes or retirement homes with several buildings. I get lost so often that my family decided to attach a compass to my car in hopes that I would always find my way home - eventually. I feel certain your volunteers will appreciate any directions you can provide to save them time and embarrassment. (Which reminds me of a story. Just last night I went to a wedding shower. I was supposed to provide the games, so I wanted to get there a few minutes early. Now I had been to this house out in the country twice before and both times at night. But this night, it was extra dark and snowing so hard that even in the headlights, the ground and the air were the same color. I saw four or five other cars in the driveway and people were moving around inside so I felt sure this was the place. I gathered my sack of games and gifts and rang the doorbell. This nice man opened the door waiving his arm and said, "Come on in." So I did. As I put down my sack and was handing my coat to him, I asked, "Where's Dana?" He said, "Dana?" HA. I wonder how long it would have been before he asked, "Why are you here?") Let's see, my point was, your volunteers will appreciate precise directions to the widows' homes.

PHOTO

On the form, to the left of the name and address area, you will see a blank space. Here I either tape a picture of the widow or scan the picture directly onto this form on a computer. When the time comes to match up volunteers, they may recognize a widow by her picture, though they never knew her name.

CONTACT PERSON

It is very important that you get the name and phone number of someone to contact in case of an emergency. There have been times when I could not reach a widow for a day or two, only to find out that she had been in the hospital and was upset that no one had come to visit her. There was one precious lady who was in the beginning stages of Alzheimer. She had no family in our town and I really needed to let a family member know that in her confusion, she had started using a can of bug spray in place of her hair spray.

This contact person also becomes someone with whom you can become friends, minister to, witness to and invite to church. Matthew Neighbors, our Minister of Music and an anointed Sunday School teacher, always says, "They don't care how much you know, until they know how much you care."

DO YOU HAVE FAMILY IN TOWN?

This gives you an idea of how much daily or weekly help this person has and how much help is needed. Be sure and put their name and number down for a contact person.

CHILDREN

Everyone loves talking about their children. Listening to a lonely widow talk about her children allows you to learn more about the widow's personality, clues you in on other family needs and prayer requests, and it gives her a chance to talk to someone besides the cat.

ARE YOU A DIABETIC?

It is important to know if you can bring sweets over or if there are any food restrictions. It may also prove beneficial to have this information should you find during a visit the widow is acting strange. She may need medical attention due to unstable blood sugar levels.

WHERE HAVE YOU WORKED?

This was so interesting. One lady in our church was in WWII and another was a midwife. They had some great stories. It also helped me match them up with a volunteer with similar interests.

WHAT ARE YOUR HOBBIES?

Knowing if the widow likes to read or crochet or plant flowers, will help you and your volunteer find the right birthday and/or Christmas present. It also shows how active she may be and helps you match her up with a volunteer who shares the same hobbies and interests.

DO YOU NEED A RIDE TO CHURCH?

Most widows are very independent. However, when they get to be in their late seventies they usually stop driving. Now their needs have dramatically changed and they will need a ride to church, special dinners, doctor appointments, grocery shopping, etc. During this transition, she will also need some extra emotional support and encouragement. She feels like she has lost the last of her independence and now she is truly old. You need to tell her that she is still useful to the kingdom of God and share specific ways she can help someone else.

SPECIAL NEEDS/COMMENTS

Many times during a visit you will discover special needs your widow has without her telling you. One lady in our church is 92 and lives alone in a very small two-room house. She has no kitchen sink or bathtub. There is a small pipe coming out of the wall with a spigot that she uses to run water into a dishpan so she can wash dishes. But she insists that she has lived happily this way her entire life, and she has no plans to change now.

12-MONTH CHECKLIST

At the bottom of the form you will notice a 12-month checklist. This is a very handy reminder to see, at a glance, if you have made contact with your widow each month. Most volunteers place this Profile either on their refrigerator or in their Bible - the two places we should all enter daily.

ORGANIZING THE NOTEBOOK

After you've gone to each home and filled out a profile for each widow, you type them all up, attach a picture to each profile, then you should make four copies of each. Place them either alphabetically in a 3-ring notebook, or color-code them geographically by North, South, East and West sides of town. If volunteers adopt a widow who lives close to their neighborhood, it will be more convenient to stop and check on them or deliver a meal. And the more convenient it is, the more often they will visit.

The information and the widows on your lists will change frequently. You will lose some precious ones, and you will gain some new ones. The best way to keep up with all the changes is to keep your widows' list on a computer.

One lady wrote and told me that the ladies in her little church had never been organized and did not see the need for it now. Hmmm, I've heard that before. Well, the only person who needs to be organized is the person in charge of the lists. You keep it up to date and simply hand the volunteer a new Widow Profile if anything has changed for the one widow they have agreed to visit. Just smile as you hand them the new sheet and say, "Bless your heart. Thank you for all you do for this sweet widow." And let the Lord do the rest!

THE "ADOPTION" PROCESS

Now here is the neat part. You go to each Sunday School Class and tell them you are asking for volunteers to "adopt" a widow. You take out a profile page with a picture on it and hold it up, tell a story about this widow, then ask someone to adopt her. The people can pass it around and see her picture, and they get so excited. Ask each volunteer to keep the Profile on their refrigerator or in their Bible and try to either call or send a card each week, and make a visit at least once a month. One lady who recently lost her husband of 60 years told her son, "Guess what? I've been adopted!" It was so cute.

Tell them you would like each widow to be adopted by at least two or three families. That way if one family misses a month contacting her, or is away on vacation, someone will still be checking on her. One sweet lady in her eighties told me that she was afraid she would die and no one would find her for days. They have these fears and need the reassurance that someone will miss them. She and a neighbor across the street now have a signal they use. Each morning she gets up and raises the window shade halfway. If her neighbor does not see the shade raised, she immediately checks on her.

There are several reasons to have two or three families adopt each widow. People come and go in the church because of job transfers, or because they are hot and cold or immature in their walk with the Lord. Also, some widows and volunteers will just hit it off and fall in love with each other, while other volunteers will only send an occasional card.

All of my grandparents have passed away and I miss that relationship that was so special as an adult. Through adopting a widow, you can once again have that special one-on-one time with a precious elderly person who needs you as much as you need her or him.

One woman in our church had spent a lot of time caring for her elderly mother. When her mother passed away, it left a big void. I was thrilled when she called and asked if she could adopt a widow. She went once a week and washed the widow's hair, rolled it and combed it out. This particular widow had only one son who lived thirty miles away and only came over every other weekend to buy groceries and check on her. When she was out of milk or bread or coffee, she had to do without until he stopped by again. Now she had a woman she could talk to, who lovingly fixed her hair and made her feel special and pretty and loved. They lived only a few blocks apart, and the volunteer would call a couple of times a week saying she was on the way to the grocery store and would love to pick something up for her. God is so good.

VOLUNTEER LIST

Be sure to ask each volunteer to sign the Volunteer List. **[Volunteer List - Appendix 2]** This way you have a record of who has adopted each widow. Later you can send them letters of encouragement and provide them with new ideas. You can also call them if you hear the widow is in the hospital, or they can call you.

You also need to call each widow and let her know who has adopted her. This way she will be expecting a call from her volunteer and won't be afraid to talk to them or let them in the house.

VOLUNTEERS

A word of caution is due here. Never adopt a widow to anyone who is not an established member of your church. We need to protect these precious older saints from con artists and deceivers who might steal from them or worse. I once had a lady call from another town who said she "wanted to take a load off my hands and look after a widow." My spirit immediately bristled against that idea and after talking to her, I learned that she had been fired from a nursing home because she "got too close to them" - whatever that meant. I thanked her for her call, but insisted that only established members of our church had the privilege of adopting a widow to love. I suggested that she read her Bible daily and pray and consider getting involved in a program in her own church or take food to an elderly neighbor.

WIDOWERS AND WIDOWS

WIDOWERS

Once again, I remind you that I use the term widow and widower interchangeably to mean any person whose spouse has died. Generally, widowers are very proud and independent so it is much harder to find out their needs. Also, I find that men tend to cry more and grieve longer. One precious widower whose wife had died two years earlier, cried every Sunday at church. I thought he had an eye ailment until I realized these were tears from grieving. His emotions were still so raw that a combination of sitting alone and listening to the songs that touched his heart, made him cry. Widowers need male companionship to talk "man talk" with and swap fish stories, but they also grieve for the understanding heart and nurturing tenderness of a woman. We need couples to invite the lonely widower into their home and provide him with a good meal and loving fellowship. Also, his hands and fingers are usually big and not accustomed to working with small things like buttons. When caring for a widower, think about tasks he had always counted on his wife to handle, such as:

1.   Sew on a button;
2.   Write thank you cards or Christmas cards;
3.   Clean out the refrigerator;
4.   Organize plastic containers in the cabinets;

31

5.   Leave meals in dishes he can heat in the microwave; and

6.   Run errands such as delivering dishes back to the church.

WIDOWS

Whether a person is a widow or widower, their needs are different from those of senior adult couples. Couples still have each other. Take my parents for example, one can't walk and the other can't remember things – due to suffering two strokes. But together, they make a whole and get along fairly well. They play cards, laugh at movies together, fuss and tease about how old the other one is, but that helps get them through their long days. It takes both of them to find where mom left her hearing aid this time. But a widow has lost that companionship, the reliance on the other's memory or stronger legs to do simple chores. They no longer experience the little pat on the hand from someone they spent the last fifty to sixty years with, each and every day. They have no one to calm their fears during a thunderstorm or tell them everything will be all right when they feel sad.

Many of the widows are in their 70's 80's and 90's. They can't climb on a chair to change a light bulb or get a blanket down from the closet. You can call and ask if there is anything they need and they will say, "Oh no. I'm just fine, thank you." But if you go over and sit and visit, you might see a light bulb out and ask if you can replace it for her. Then she will let you and be very thankful for your help.

We live in a small town about twenty miles from Tulsa.

One very sweet lady was paying a woman in town $20 to take her to Tulsa to the doctor. That just broke my heart. Here she was sick and on a very limited income and having to pay money for the doctor's visit, medication and now $20 for a ride. I told her not to ever pay for help again. Now we have volunteers from our church who do not work during the day and are happy to take these widows to a doctor's appointment in Tulsa. They usually eat out and make a fun day of it. And the best part is hearing all their wonderful stories about life 70 years ago.

SPIRITUAL NEEDS

Never assume that just because someone is old, that they have had a personal relationship with Jesus. It is possible they have gone to church all their lives, but never asked Jesus to come into their heart and save them. Always, at some point, ask them to tell you about their salvation experience. You will be blessed by their testimonies and both of you will be reassured about their salvation. I try to keep their stories in a journal and make a note of those who may not have ever had a true salvation experience. Some stories are such blessings to hear and share.

WINTER

During the winter months, when the wind is cold and blowing, these elderly people do not need to be outside. When a winter storm hits and there is ice or snow on the ground for a week at a time, please remember to call and get grocery lists from them. Many times they run out of bread and meat.

Delivering a few groceries may keep someone from falling and breaking a hip or getting pneumonia. At one apartment complex, all the washers and dryers are in a little building attached to the back of each apartment and the tenants have to go outside to enter the laundry room. My husband and I went to each widow's apartment and shoveled snow off the sidewalk and made sure a light bulb was hung properly so the washers wouldn't freeze up. They had many people they could have called, but did not. You see, most widows and widowers alike are too independent and proud to ask for help. Don't wait until they ask. Go and tell them you are there to help and just do it.

One lady said she was so tired of sitting day and night in her apartment. When I asked where she would like to go, she said she would love to see the Christmas lights. What fun it was to drive her around Tulsa to look at all the beautifully decorated houses and sparkling lights.

It always amazes me how even widows with family close by, spend holidays alone. Some families are "just too busy" to have this old person under their feet. So never assume that because a widow has family in town that she will go there for Thanksgiving Dinner or for Christmas. Invite a widow plus a friend of hers to come to Thanksgiving Dinner with your family. It will be a witness to the widow's friend who may not go to church anywhere. It is also a witness to your own family and children that they will remember all their lives.

When I was growing up, my mother was always fixing meals for someone who was sick, and it was very common for us to have extra people over for dinner. But many young women today have not had that example to follow. They haven't grown up in Christian homes and need to be taught the joy of serving others. Many of the widows worked in the church serving others all their lives and now it is time to serve them.

One such lady in our widows group is actually not a widow. She never married. She spent her entire life working in the church and teaching Sunday School. Now in her eighties, she still drives to the nursing home and to homes of shut-ins each week to read them their Sunday School lesson. What an example to all of us.

Philippians 2:1-4 says this, [1]"If you have any encouragement from being united with Christ, if any comfort from his love, if any fellowship with the Spirit, if any tenderness and compassion, [2]then make my joy complete by being like-minded, having the same love, being one in spirit and purpose. [3]Do nothing out of selfish ambition or vain conceit, but in humility consider others better than yourselves. [4]Each of you should look not only to your own interest, but also to the interests of others."

SPRING

Now the winter months are passing and they will need help putting the extra blankets up in a closet they can't reach. It is a time of refreshing and new life. Offer to take the widow for a ride through the park to watch the children play. Take her, in her car, to the car wash and drive it through for her. Many of them are afraid of driving through an automatic car wash, but will appreciate having their car washed and vacuumed.

SUMMER

During the hot summer months, how many times have you cut a watermelon and found that you just did not have room for the whole thing in your refrigerator? Take a piece of watermelon in a pie plate to a widow. She will love the watermelon and the pie plate will keep the juice from spilling. Hang a basket of flowers on her front porch and go by each week to water it for her while you visit.

FALL

They may need help covering the windows of older homes with heavy plastic or wrapping an air conditioner so the cold wind doesn't blow in.

THEY JUST NEED TO BE LOVED ON

No matter what the season, winter, spring, summer or fall, widows need to be loved. Love and hugs are two things you can give away, yet never run out of a fresh supply. Widows also need nutritional food. One small widow could hardly justify cooking a pot roast with potatoes and carrots. It is hard to cook a nutritious meal for one. So please remember when you fix a big meal for your family, to fill an extra plate and take it to a widow.

Then nourish their soul by reading the Bible to them. Even John the Baptist, when in prison, needed reassurance. Reassure them that God is in control.

WHAT YOU CAN DO

- Sit by them at church so they don't feel alone
- Pick them up for special dinners or church functions
- Invite them to share Sunday dinner with your family
- Give them lots and lots of hugs
- Send birthday cards and cards of encouragement
- Tell them you love them
- Ask their advice on how to take care of a plant
- Take a plate of food by for their supper
- Take a plate of homemade cookies over with a fresh jug of milk
- Read the Bible to them
- Be available and let them know they can call you for help

WHAT CAN A WIDOW DO?

1.   PRAY

Widows have extra time to spend in prayer, and the experience and faith to very effective prayer partners.   Tell them your prayer requests and ask them to pray for you and your family. Ask them to be your prayer partners. This will have a dual effect: (1) it will make them feel needed and help you develop a bond with each other, and (2) they will be strengthened from their time spent in prayer with the Lord.

2.   SEND CARDS and BE AN ENCOURAGER

Their wisdom and encouragement will mean so much to a pastor, music director, Sunday School teacher, or a friend. Take your widow a box of greeting cards and put postage stamps on each envelope. Then in large print, list the name and address of workers in your church who may need a word of encouragement. Everyone receives a blessing. This is also a gentle reminder for her to be an encourager and not a gossiper.

3.   MENTOR YOUNGER WOMEN

Psalm 71:18 says, "Even when I am old and gray, do not forsake me, O God, till I declare your power to the next generation, your might to all who are to come.
Remind them that they can be witnesses to their neighbors and

to younger women at church, including their volunteer who has adopted them. I have to tell you about one of our widows, Esther. Every time I get a chance to sit down and visit with her, she tells me about her prayer "conversations" with God at the breakfast table. Without fail, through all her daily adventures and struggles with cancer, she always says, "Well, it's just you and me again, God. No one else can do anything with me." I love Esther. No matter what I'm going through, because of Esther's testimony, I am reminded that it all comes down to "just you and me, God." And I go to Him in prayer.

4. SIMPLY HOLD AND ROCK THE BABIES IN THE NURSERY

Encourage a widow to volunteer to hold and rock the babies in the nursery. Be certain that younger women are working to take care of the babies, change diapers and do the work, but let the widow sit and cuddle the babies and rock them to sleep. It will be good for both of them.

5. ASK THEM TO PUT TOGETHER A BOOK OF WISDOM

Gather their old sayings or stories of faith or poems and put them together in a book. Some churches put together cookbooks for sale. Why not put together a book of wisdom? If you offer them for sale, use the money for an appreciation banquet, to buy flowers for each widow, or to add to a fix-it fund.

NURSING HOMES

I have to tell you a story about a precious lady named Minnie Thompson. Minnie was only 4 feet tall, but she was a prayer warrior even in her nineties! She was able to stay in her own little home till she was 93 years old. When she came close to burning the house down and forgetting her medicine daily, they put her in a nursing home. At 96 years of age, she went to be with the Lord. One of the last times I visited Minnie in the nursing home, she was sitting in the dining room clutching her purse. She looked up and said, "Can you get me out of here?" which wasn't like her at all. I sat down by her and said, "No, Minnie, I can't. But I'll sit with you a while and hold your hand." Then I reminded her that her heavenly father loved her. A peace and joy came over her face and she said to me so clear minded, "My father told me about Jesus when I was a little girl. And I can still see him playing out in the yard with us children." Then she said, "That's what's wrong with people today, somebody forgot to tell them about Jesus." Oh that went right to my heart, to think that this 96-year-old woman had the answer to life's problems - Jesus. Her life is a testimony that God is faithful to the end. Now instead of complaining about the shape of the world or how awful someone might be, I just think "somebody forgot to tell them about Jesus."

Each of us needs to take this to heart and tell someone about Jesus. Oh the wisdom of the aged saints of God. You see,

no matter how old they are, they can be an encourager to anyone who will take the time to listen.

Men in nursing homes really appreciate another man
stopping by to play checkers or swap fish stories. They also
long to have the Bible read to them and have others pray for
them.

GETTING EVERYONE INVOLVED

CHILDREN

Old people love children. Maybe it is because children remind them of their youth, or maybe it's because it makes them feel joyful watching little ones play. Occasionally (and I say occasionally because too much of a good thing can make them nervous, especially if the children are noisy) the volunteers might take their young children for a brief visit. Some widows love it and ask you to bring them often. But be sensitive to their feelings.

Another great way to get children involved is to go to the preschool class, or if your church actually has a school, go to the first grade class. Ask the teacher for her class to adopt a widow. Then once a month the children can color pictures or cut out paper crosses. On the widow's birthday, they can all sign a birthday card in their precious little handwriting. The teacher can give them a lesson about older people. Then the children stop and pray for this widow before sending the card. The children have learned a valuable lesson and the widow receives a blessing as well.

YOUTH

One thing four or five of the widows had mentioned was how much they missed having beautiful flower beds after their husbands died. Their husbands had always cleaned and tilled the ground and planted flowers every summer. So one summer I asked our youth to meet at the church on a Saturday morning and bring rakes, grass clippers, weed-eaters, etc. They piled into the back of pickup trucks and I dropped teams of four teenagers off at a few different widows' houses. We all went to the door, and I introduced them to her explaining that we had come to rake and clean out her flower beds. Then we bought flowers and planted them. At one house we even rebuilt a broken trellis. The kids had such a great time that a couple of them went back each month to check on the flowers and visit with the widows. It was a witness to the whole neighborhood to see the youth from our church helping these ladies. And the widows enjoyed telling their neighbors, "My church did this for me."

WOMEN

One of our ladies' church groups is called Journey. You see, each of us is on our own "journey" learning to serve and grow in the Lord. Our Journey group provides three or four different opportunities for women to choose each month what road of service they want to take. I try to present a different opportunity each month for them to serve our widows. One month we all brought little bottles of lotions, shampoos and soaps you get when you stay in a hotel. We put them in small white sacks and tied pretty ribbons on them. Then a couple of volunteers took them to the different nursing homes and to each of our widows. One young lady said she cried all the way home - she was so touched by the way their faces lit up. She had never experienced the joy of giving to someone who was so lonely.

Some of our ladies who crochet and knit made small Afghans and delivered them to our widows in nursing homes. The widows were so proud of the soft, warm Afghans, and told everyone that their church made them. Last Christmas, we started a quilting project. I taught a "Quilting Class 101" to women who had never quilted before and to the 7th and 8th grade girls. Between those groups and all the ladies who already knew how to quilt, we made 34 lap-size quilts and delivered one to each of our widows and widowers.

One summer I asked the women in our church choir for donations, and we took a pot of flowers or a hanging basket to each widow. Even the widows living in retirement complexes could set a small basket of flowers on their porches. There is just something about a basket of flowers that lifts your spirit.

Another time we invited any woman interested to meet on February 12th and bring leftover children's Valentine cards and a dozen homemade cookies. We put a white doily on bright red plates then covered them with assorted homemade cookies. Then we wrapped each plate in pink cellophane and tied bows and ribbons around them. I had labels made up with each widow's name, address and telephone number which we stuck to each plate with a child's Valentine card signed "from the ladies of First Baptist Church". Each woman selected a couple of plates to deliver by February 14th. We made extras because there were a few elderly couples who needed the encouragement and to be loved on as well.

One lady took her Bible with her to visit a homebound widow. She asked if there was anything the widow would especially like to hear read from the Bible. The very elderly widow said she remembered hearing her mother read Psalm 23 to her and the 10 commandments. So the volunteer sat and read the Bible to her. How sweet to hear the Word of God read since she was nearly blind and could not read it for herself.

A new widow who was recently adopted said she was having such a hard time after her husband died, but at just the right moment here would come another card of encouragement that brightened her day. So you see, you could recruit some women just for sending cards.

CHRISTMAS — ANGEL TREE

My husband made a large stand and attached a 4' x 6' piece of plywood. We taped a Christmas Tree plastic door cover on the front then screwed gold cup hooks all over it. On each hook we hung several bright envelopes with Christmas stickers on them and the name of a widow on the front. Inside each envelope I placed a Christmas card and a piece of paper that listed that widow's name, address, phone number and a wish list with two or three $5.00 items. I had called each widow and asked what she would like for Christmas and they all said things like lotion, gloves, slippers, postage stamps, a book, etc.

Then at our Thanksgiving Dinner I put this Angel Tree up by the door and asked people to take an envelope off and buy one gift that was on the widow's wish list. They were to wrap the gift and go with their family to deliver the gift before Christmas. All the envelopes were gone by the next Sunday. I had so many reports of how much the people were blessed by this visit with a widow. Now we put up an angel tree each Christmas in our church.

You can vary the angel tree. One Christmas we decorated a basket and laid the envelopes in the basket on the alter for people to come by and pick up at the end of the Christmas service. Then last year we attached the names and wish lists to Christmas tree ornaments and they picked the ornament off of a Christmas tree on the stage.

We also had a fancy luncheon/tea for Christmas for the widows. We assigned ladies to pick up three or four widows each and bring them to a beautiful home on the lake. We played games, gave them each a little gift and served a beautiful lunch. We even invited a few of their friends who did not attend church anywhere. We had a lovely time, and the widows witnessed to their friends.

SUNDAY SCHOOL CLASSES

One adult Sunday School class adopted a widow who had very little family left. They brought a large basket to class in November. Then all through December they brought little wrapped gifts and a new blanket. On Christmas Eve, several class members went together and delivered the basket full of goodies and sang Christmas carols.

This same Sunday School class built a new porch for a widow whose porch was falling down.

Another widow didn't stop her car in time and put a hole in the sheet rock of her garage. A couple of retired handymen got together and repaired the sheet rock.

The main thing to remember is this, you will never know they have these needs if you don't visit them and talk to them on a regular basis. They just will not ask for help.

CHURCH SERVICES

One more idea is to have a widow's night at church. You could have a short devotional or short sermon on one of the several stories in the Bible about how God has provided for widows. Then ask three or four widows to prepare and sing a song. You could ask two or three widows and their volunteers who adopted them, to give their testimony.

OLDER WOMEN TO MENTOR THE YOUNG ONES

Ask a widow to come to a young married women's class and talk to them about marriage. The younger women will have so much fun hearing stories of how they use to wash clothes in the creek, work a garden and take care of young babies - all at the same time.

One widow told a story about when she and her husband had a terrible fight, but they worked it out and went right on loving each other. They were married sixty years before he passed away.

One widowed man said he didn't talk to his wife for two years... because he didn't want to interrupt her! HA. **Proverbs 17:22, "A cheerful heart is good medicine, but a crushed spirit dries up the bones."**

They will make you laugh and cry with their wonderful

stories. I haven't figured out who gets the biggest blessing, the widow or the volunteer.

MEN

You may want to have a car service day and tell the widows they can bring their car to the church on Saturday and the men will change their oil and vacuum their cars.

DEACONS

I also made up a quick chart **[Quick Chart - Appendix 3]** showing the name, address, phone number and 12-month check list and attached another sheet showing all widow's birthdays. I keep this updated each month and give a copy to each deacon. This list is also given to our women's Journey group and WMU who want to send birthday cards each month. Some people don't have time to make visits but they will commit to sending a card of encouragement each month or a birthday card to each widow.

Once a month our deacons go to shut-ins homes and observe the Lord's Supper with them and have Bible reading and prayer.

ORGANIZATION
Notebook, Card File, Computer

NOTEBOOK OR 3-RING BINDER

Now to tie it all together, you need to keep a large binder **[Notebook - Appendix 4]** with four copies of each widow's profile behind alphabetical tabs. At the front of your binder, you will want to put the chart listing each widow and their volunteers. This way you can tell at a glance who still needs to be adopted. Also, if you hear a widow is sick or in the hospital, you can look quickly and see which volunteers you need to notify.

I also keep a list of birthdays so I can address birthday cards for the entire month, then send them out on time. You should also keep a list of ladies who do not work during the day, who have volunteered to take the widows to the doctor.

Just to be sure you understand, your notebook should contain the following:

1. **Chart with Widows' names, addresses, volunteer and widows' phone numbers;**
2. **Chart of volunteers' names, addresses, phone numbers and who they adopted;**
3. **Chart of birthdays;**
4. **List of volunteers who are available to transport widows to doctors' appointments;**

5. **Alphabetical tabs with four copies of each widow's profile sheets;**

6. **Record of visit behind each Widow's Profile; and**

7. **Supply of Volunteer Orientation sheet you can give to each new volunteer.**

As with any good program, you must stay in contact with your volunteers to encourage them and keep them informed and actively involved. **[Letters - Appendix 5]** So, three or four times a year I send new ideas or seasonal reminders of widows' needs. Also, to keep your volunteers encouraged, send stories of feedback you have received telling how happy and grateful the widows are.

If you have the time and equipment, a monthly newsletter would be a great idea. You could put in pictures of widows and volunteers together. You could have a section telling what opportunities are coming up or report on a finished project. Remember the old saying, "Out of sight, out of mind." Well, the more you publish what is happening, the more other people will want to join in and then everyone is blessed.

CARD FILE

If you prefer to keep things simple and don't have the means to keep a chart updated, a very simple, yet organized, approach is to keep a set of 3 x 5 index cards in a file box. You simply glue or tape a widow's picture on a 3 x 5 index card and write her or his name at the top. You have lines below to write their name, address, phone number and the name of who adopted them. You can write a note to yourself on the back of the card, (i.e., "she likes apple pie") or keep a diary of your visits.

COMPUTER SOFTWARE PROGRAM

If you have a computer and your lists seem to be constantly changing, you really should keep files on the computer. I keep all my lists on the computer, which makes it easy to update and print copies for the deacons.

SERVICE AND LOVE

One last bit of advice from the Bible. Okay, maybe two or three bits. No one should adopt a widow out of guilt or duty or pressure. But everyone should try it at least once, out of love.

Giving your time is like giving your tithe. I know this is a very busy, fast-paced world we live in today, but when you give to God, He has a way of multiplying and returning a blessing. Just as Jesus blessed the two small fishes and five small loaves of barley the little boy gave, and was able to feed five thousand, God will bless and miraculously multiply the time you give till it seems like you have more time. Have you ever tried to give a tenth of your time, just as you give a tenth of your money?

I Peter 4:11 says this, ". . . If anyone serves, he should do it with the strength God provides, so that in all things God may be praised through Jesus Christ..."

2 Corinthians 9:6-8 "Remember this: Whoever sows sparingly will also reap sparingly, and whoever sows generously will also reap generously. Each man should give what he has decided in his heart to give, not reluctantly or under compulsion, for God loves a cheerful giver. And God is able to make all grace abound to you, so that in all things at all times, having all that you need, you will abound in every good work."

Whether you are an individual reading this to learn how

to help one widow, or if you want to start this program in your church and involve sixty widows, may God bless you and so fill you with His love that it overflows into the lives of others, that He might be glorified.

WIDOW / WIDOWER / HOMEBOUND / PROFILE

Name	
Address	
Directions	
Phone No.	
Birthday	

Contact Person / Phone No.	
Do you have family in town?	
Children?	
Are you a diabetic?	
Where have you worked?	
What are your hobbies?	
Do you need a ride to church?	
Needs/Comments	

Your life is a living testimony that God is faithful.

	Jan	Feb	Mar	Apr	May	Jun	Jul	Aug	Sep	Oct	Nov	Dec
Visits												
Calls												
Cards												

57

RECORD OF VISITS	
Date	*Comments*

VOLUNTEER LIST

	Name	Address	Widow	Phone
1				
2				
3				
4				
5				
6				
7				
8				
9				
10				
11				
12				
13				
14				
15				
16				
17				
18				
19				
20				
21				
23				
24				

Widows Birthdays

JANUARY	FEBRUARY	MARCH	APRIL
MAY	JUNE	JULY	AUGUST
SEPTEMBER	OCTOBER	NOVEMBER	DECEMBER

Revised

WIDOWS LIST

	Name	Address	Phone	Jan	Feb	Mar	Apr	May	Jun	Jul	Aug	Sep	Oct	Nov	Dec
1															
2															
3															
4															
5															
6															
7															
8															
9															
10															
11															
12															
13															
14															
15															
16															

QUICK CHARTS

Widows List

	Name	Address	Volunteer	Widow Phone
1				
2				
3				
4				
5				
6				
7				
8				
9				
10				
11				
12				
13				
14				

WIDOWS BIRTHDAYS

JANUARY	JULY
FEBRUARY	AUGUST
MARCH	SEPTEMBER
APRIL	OCTOBER
MAY	NOVEMBER
JUNE	DECEMBER

VOLUNTEER LIST

	Name	Address	Widow	Phone
1				
2				
3				
4				
5				
6				
7				
8				
9				
10				
11				
12				
13				
14				
15				
16				
17				
18				
19				
20				
21				
22				
23				
24				
25				

	Volunteer	Phone	Notes

WIDOW / WIDOWER / HOMEBOUND / PROFILE

Name	
Address	
Directions	
Phone No.	

Contact Person / Phone No.	
Do you have family in town?	
Children?	
Are you a diabetic?	
Where have you worked?	
What are your hobbies?	
Do you need a ride to church?	
Needs/Comments	

Your life is a living testimony that God is faithful.

	Jan	Feb	Mar	Apr	May	Jun	Jul	Aug	Sep	Oct	Nov	Dec
Visits												
Calls												
Cards												

RECORD OF VISITS

Date	Comments

VOLUNTEER ORIENTATION

Thank you so much for volunteering. Most of these people have been faithful to the Lord and our church most of their lives. Some have not. But one thing they all have in common is that they are widows or widowers. This has caused a void in their lives intensified by the fact that they are in the latter years of their lives. They need to know someone cares about them. They need to be loved and needed. Some have family in town that call and check on them regularly, but some of them have no family here at all. And family can't be there all the time. The following are some of the things they have said to me that will give you a little more insight into how they feel.

1. "I'm afraid I'll die and no one will know and I won't be found for 3 or 4 days."
2. "I used to be so independent and drove to Tulsa every day just to get out. Now I can't drive in Tulsa and I just want to get out for 15 minutes to see the flowers."
3. I can't drive in Tulsa anymore and a woman in town charges $20 a trip to take us to the doctor.
4. No one ever comes to see me anymore.
5. Can't clean very well because of my knee.
6. I can't get down and vacuum the car out so I pay $30 to have someone clean it inside and out.
7. I can't plant flowers anymore. My husband used to do that and I sure miss seeing the pretty flowers.
8. I just need a hug now and then.

Please take time to call and tell them you're thinking about them. If any of them have a doctor's appointment in Tulsa and don't have a ride, let me know. We have four volunteers who are willing and happy to take them. Also, please call me if you find out they are going into the hospital. The following are suggestions:

1. Take a morning walk with them if you don't work.
2. Take them cookies.
3. Send them a cheerful card of encouragement.
4. If you cook a big pot of beans and cornbread, take them a little dish. If they are sick, it is hard for them to cook nourishing meals.
5. Go speak to them at church on Sunday morning. They sit in the same seat every Sunday.
6. DON'T TELL WHAT THEY HAVE SAID. Some things need to be kept confidential.
7. Don't patronize them or treat them like children. Treat them with respect and dignity.
8. Ask them questions about what they did in life, how they met their husband, where they lived, how they handled certain problems back then. They love to reminisce and they have wonderful real life stories.
9. Remind them that God is not finished with them yet. Tell them you appreciate their faithfulness to this church and to the Lord.
10. Above all, love them. They'll feel it and know it, and it will make a difference.

Some of our younger or more independent widows have requested only phone calls or cards. For those of you who have volunteered in this area, please try to call or send a card once a week. Through your phone calls we find out that some are sick or in the hospital. Please pass this information on to me so that others can visit them.

Thank you so much for your time. May God bless you as you give to others. The fruit of the spirit is love, joy, peace, longsuffering, kindness, goodness, faithfulness, gentleness, self-control. May you grow in the spirit of the Lord as you allow God to work through you as you visit and call these precious people.

Dear Volunteers:

Thank you so much for your help. I have heard many wonderful reports of your kindness to the widows in our church. Every card you send, every phone call and each visit fills their hearts with joy at the thought that someone still cares about them.

Pure and undefiled religion before God and the Father is this: to visit orphans and widows in their trouble, and to keep oneself unspotted from the world.

James 1:27

School will be starting soon and some of you will have extra time on your hands with the kids gone all day. Please try to visit your widow. Some of you have gotten really close to your ladies and say they seem like an adopted grandmother. What a blessing you are to each other.

I know sometimes people just don't hit it off and if this has happened with you please feel free to call me and ask to change to another person. You might want to request someone who has a hobby you can both share such as flowers or a love for books, history or chocolate!

THIS MONTH I would like to ask you to remember that many of these ladies have knee trouble or don't balance well and it is not only a chore, but dangerous for them to try and change a light bulb in the ceiling. It would only take a few minutes for you to stop by their house (with a package of light bulbs) and replace their burned out bulbs. I've found that if you ask them over the phone, they will just say they don't need any-thing because they don't want to be a bother to you. If you show up with bulbs in hand, they will gladly agree and appreciate it so much.

Don't forget to call me when you hear of someone in the hospital or feeling bad. I love to cook and many times have leftovers that I end up throwing out. So now as I clear the table, I fill an extra plate and take it by someone's house. It's amaz-ing how God just lays someone on my heart to take it to and then I find out they haven't been feeling well. I know if I'm the only one home some night for dinner that I tend to just snack and not fix a nutritious meal. These ladies face that problem every day. Please remember to share your leftovers with some-one this month.

Thank you again and may God richly bless you for your kindness.

Dear Volunteers,

Spring is here and summer is on its way! What a beautiful time to share your love with our widows. I have heard so many wonderful praises about the birthday cards they have received and acts of kindness. With the change in where we meet for worship services, please try to find the widow you have adopted and give them a hug or sit by them on Sunday mornings.

The widows ministry started almost four years ago. During that time, we have lost some precious saints. We have also acquired some new widows that need our love so much during this time of sorrow, loneliness and adjustment.

Pure and undefiled religion before God and the Father is this: to visit orphans and widows in their trouble, and to keep oneself unspotted from the world.

James 1:27

Thank you all for being so faithful to remember to call or visit. However, I would like to enlighten you about some needs you may not be aware of. For a person in their 80's and 90's, four years can make quite a difference. Someone that was driving and getting around independently a couple of years ago may be needing a ride to church now. A couple of our ladies have lost their drivers license and car and need help getting groceries. Please remember also that they don't eat well because they don't feel like standing up cooking due to illness, arthritis in their knees and just not having the energy anymore.

But this I say: He who sows sparingly will also reap sparingly, and he who sows bountifully will also reap bountifully. So let each one give as he purposes in his heart, not grudgingly or of necessity; for God loves a cheerful giver. And God is able to make all grace abound toward you, that you, always having all sufficiency in all things, may have an abundance for every good work

2 Corinthians 9:6-9

Isn't it amazing how God multiplies your time when you give your time to Him. I was rushing around a couple of Saturdays ago and felt drawn to stop at the Skiatook Nursing Home. I kept telling myself that I was too busy and there just wasn't time. But about two blocks past it, I turned around and went back. There was little Minnie Thompson and the first words out of her mouth were "Can you get me out of here." Bless her heart, she was having a bad day; and I hope in some small way I helped. I reminded her of how much the Lord loved her and I loved her. I hugged her and held her hand as we talked about when she was a little girl playing in the yard with her daddy. Then she started telling me about how people needed to tell their kids about Jesus. What a blessing she was to me. Not only did I get everything accomplished on my "to do" list, but my attitude was changed for the rest of the day. I felt so blessed and loved and ready to love others. Jesus said:

"Inasmuch as you have done it unto one of the least of these my brethren, you have done it unto me."

Matthew 25:40

Thank you so much for all that you are doing. There is an old song that comes to mind, "They will know we are Christians by our love." May your love abound.

Author Contact Information

Contact Vicki Hendryx or order more copies of this book at

TATE PUBLISHING, LLC

1716 West State Highway 152
Mustang, Oklahoma 73064

(888) 361 - 9473

www.tatepublishing.com

ABOUT VICKI HENDRYX

Vicki Hendryx has lived in a small town in Northeastern Oklahoma for 50 years where four generations of her family have been raised. She has taught many Sunday School classes and is involved in the intercessory prayer group. Vicki found her true calling when the Lord led her to begin a widow ministry to the many lonely widowed and elderly people in her church and community.

She is an adult literacy volunteer, a federal judicial secretary, takes care of her elderly parents, and enjoys spending time with her husband Jerry at the softball fields since both of her children have recently married.

Like many of you, her life is very busy, but she finds her strength and her joy in serving the Lord and says, "Our time is like our tithe. When you give it to the Lord, He blesses and multiplies in ways that cannot be explained."

Vicki Hendryx has been a guest speaker at several seminars on ministry to senior adults and her enthusiasm and practical solutions are both motivating and heartwarming.

To each person who receives this manual, my prayer is that you do all in the name of Jesus that the Father might be glorified. I look forward to hearing from you about how God is blessing your church. Remember not to look back at what someone has tried in the past, not to look left or right at what others are doing, but to look up. Help is only a prayer away.

"The Joy of the Lord is your strength."
Nehemiah 8:10

Vicki
widowsministry@yahoo.com